Discover The Process That Will Make You Shine

Written By

Edna L Isaac

Copyright © 2025 by Edna L Isaac

ISBN 978-1-938432-42-2

Refined Like Gold written by Edna L Isaac

All rights reserved.

No portion of this book may be reproduced in any form without written permission from the publisher or author, except as permitted by U.S. copyright law.

Front and back cover designed by JDN Publications, image on cover created with Magic Media in Canva.

isaacednaliz (Creator). (2025, April). *gold only theliquid* [AI-generated image]. Canva, Magic Media.

Disclaimer

JDN Publications/EDUCATE Publishing is a self-publishing platform that offers authors the opportunity to publish their works without the need to go through an editorial selection process. Authors are responsible for the content of their works, and in particular, JDN/EDUCATE does not necessarily agree with the content of this book. We are not responsible for errors herein, and we assume no liability for the consequences of reading it. Readers should be aware that the content of this book is the sole responsibility of the author.

Printed in the United States of America

TABLE OF CONTENTS

DEDICATION	V
PROLOGUE	VII
INTRODUCTION	XI
CHAPTER 1	1
CHAPTER 2	7
CHAPTER 3	15
CHAPTER 4	23
CHAPTER 5	33
CHAPTER 6	37
CHAPTER 7	47
CHAPTER 8	55
CHAPTER 9	63
CONCLUSION	69
ABOUT THE AUTHOR	75
REFERENCES	79

DEDICATION

WITH DEEP GRATITUDE

I dedicate this book to the Father, Son, and Holy Spirit, source of all inspiration and strength. And to you, my beloved mother, Edith Olga Román, my "Mami," whose unconditional love has been the beacon that guided my life and that of my siblings as we grew up.

Thank you, Mami, for being the living example of a hardworking, fighting, kind, and humble woman. Your greatness resides in anonymity, in selfless service, and total dedication to others. You have sacrificed so much, expecting nothing in return, demonstrating a generosity that inspires all who know you. I will never forget your tireless efforts, those long walks under the sun to ensure the sustenance of our family.

Thank you, a thousand thanks, for every step, for every sacrifice. I am grateful for the solid foundation of morality and respect that you have instilled in us, values that endure and that we hope to transmit to future generations. Your most precious legacy, the knowledge of Jesus Christ, our King and Savior, is the greatest treasure you have given me. If I could choose again, I would choose you a thousand times over as my mother.

I love you, Mami, with all my being. I wish you the best that life can offer!

PROLOGUE

WOULD YOU LIKE TO SHINE?

What is happening to us? What is going on? In a world where competition for attention is fierce, it's important not just to shine but to do so correctly, especially if we want to make a positive impact on children, families, and future generations, leaving behind a legacy worthy of admiration. Despite living in a time where hatred, selfishness, and disrespect seem prevalent, I believe there is still hope. We need leaders to emerge who refuse to conform to the status quo. I am confident that together, we can inspire the new generation to shine authentically. God has always intended for generations to shine according to His design. We all desire to shine like gold, to triumph, and to be examples for others. This desire is commendable, but for many, it remains just that: a desire.

No one is born to fail

From childhood, we dream of a bright future, and these dreams drive and define us. I can speak from my own experience; I grew up in a very humble household, but I often daydreamed of a perfect world with no limits, borders, or impossibilities. This positive attitude has motivated me to always seek the best version of myself. I do not aim for riches; instead, I want to leave a legacy that makes a lasting impact. We all want to shine, but the path can be challenging, and many people give up along the way.

Instead of focusing on what seems impossible, let's direct our attention to our goals, following the example of Jesus' persistence. If He overcame obstacles, so can we, but unfortunately many of us have been undisciplined and have settled for mediocrity, often resisting the urge to leave our comfort zones.

Seeking Instant Gratification

Certainly, it can be easier to live according to our fleshly desires rather than submit to the transformation that God desires for us, which requires discipline and humility. We often seek instant results without making any real effort, much like wanting to lose weight without changing our bad eating habits. However, true transformation takes time and dedication.

We often approach the Word of God selectively, applying it only when it suits our convenience. We tend to overlook passages that challenge us, such as 1 Corinthians 3:16-17, which reminds us that our bodies are temples of the Holy Spirit. Instead, we seek easy and quick solutions, wanting "get rich quick" schemes without any effort or commitment. However, Proverbs 13:4 warns us that "...the sluggard craves yet receives nothing, while the diligent are fully satisfied."

God has created us with immense potential, but our transformation relies on our willingness to engage in the process. Just like gold, we must endure refining to shine at our fullest purity and reflect God's glory. The refining of gold is a long and arduous journey; the purer the gold we desire, the more intense the process must be. Our transformation is also very intense, but it is a worthwhile endeavor.

This journey invites us to reflect on our current stage. Regardless of where we are, the important thing is not to give up, for God is with us throughout this process. In striving for transformation, we can find the answer to the question: Why can't I shine even though I yearn for it so much?

INTRODUCTION

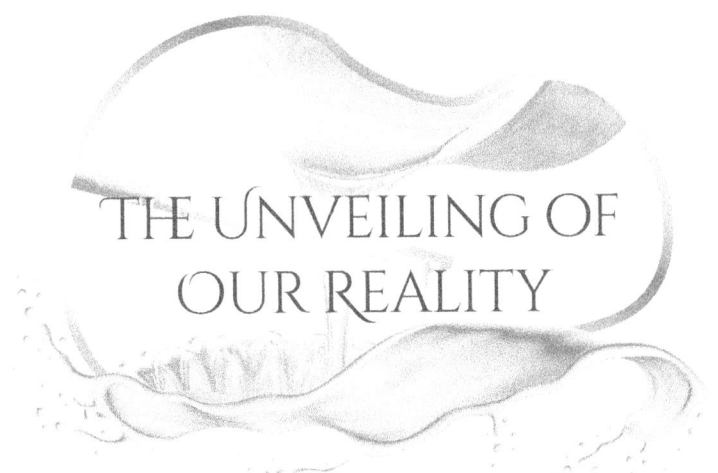

THE UNVEILING OF OUR REALITY

What times we are living in! Reality surpasses fiction, and our eyes witness unprecedented chaos. The modern era crumbles under the weight of individualism, where the "I" eclipses the "we." Courtesy dissolves in a whirlwind of sarcasm and hurtful insults, while world leaders navigate without a compass. I must admit that negativity is not my ally. However, this writing requires a candid look, even if it may seem pessimistic at the moment.

Let's be clear: there is still hope, and it resides in those hearts that yearn to shine and be a source of light—beacons of righteousness in a sea of uncertainty—willing to embrace sacrifice and injustice as steppingstones toward a higher ideal that will guide us to shine, but in the right way.

The Collapse of Decency

We have witnessed a generation fade into obscurity, disconnected from its roots and unable to honor the legacy of its ancestors. It is truly regrettable to see that we have lost almost an entire generation, with many young people unable to connect with those who came before them. Admiration for those who have forged our path is fading, and ethics are becoming relics of the past, even among the most learned. The manipulation of truth has become a weapon, and defamation masquerades as justice, all in the name of personal agendas and the lust for power. This should not be surprising, as the Word of God warned us long ago:

> This also knows that in the last days perilous times shall come. For men shall be lovers of their own selves, covetous, boasters, proud, blasphemers, disobedient to parents, unthankful, unholy. Without natural affection, trucebreakers, false accusers, incontinent, fierce, despisers of those that are good, Traitors, heady, high-minded, lovers of pleasures more than lovers of God; Having a form of

godliness but denying the power thereof: from such turn away. 2 Timothy 3:1-5 (KJV)

The twilight of decency plunges us into an abyss where obscenity is sold as medicine for the soul. How have we allowed morality and ethics to vanish from our perspective? The divine Word is being fulfilled, and darkness is disguising itself as light, while genuine light is condemned to darkness. We cannot be surprised that the "enlightened elite" embrace the abominable, for the prince of this world delights in blinding those who reject the Truth.

Not All is Lost

Amid this storm, responsibility calls us to make transcendent decisions and to keep our gaze fixed on the eternal. We were created in the image and likeness of God, destined to reflect His glory on this earth. There is still time to recover lost ground and ignite the spark within us. It requires only a burning desire and an unwavering commitment.

Join me on this journey where together we will discover how the purifying fire of refinement can transform us into brilliant gold, capable of illuminating our lives, our families, and our society. Throughout this book, we will explore the fascinating process of being refined like gold, drawing a parallel between the alchemy of this precious metal and the spiritual transformation that awaits us. Each chapter will be a step toward optimizing our being, an opportunity to shine with the light that God has placed within us.

CHAPTER 1

SHINING THE RIGHT WAY

Although we observe decay all around us, it is crucial to recognize that not all is lost; there is still hope, and we can shine with the right intentions. There is a significant need and desire for new leaders to emerge—leaders who do not conform to the crowd or the status quo. I believe that together, we can inspire our new generation to shine for themselves, but in the right way. Historically, it was always God's intention for new generations to learn to shine as He designed from the beginning, according to the Scriptures. From generation to generation, God commanded His followers to repeat His words and ensure that His precepts and statutes were taught to our descendants. Therefore, it is not merely an option—it is a mandate that we pass on the responsibility to the new generations to do things correctly.

> These commandments that I give you today are to be on your hearts. Impress them on your children. Talk about them when you sit at home and when you walk along the road, when you lie down, and when you get up. Tie them as symbols on your hands and bind them on your foreheads. Write them on the doorframes of your houses and on your gates. Deuteronomy 6:6-9

When we observe the gold, one of the most appreciated and valuable metals since ancient times, we will see that it is durable and never gets damaged. Centuries can pass, and it remains free from corrosion. Gold is persistent, shiny, and valuable; similarly, we should strive to shine for Christ and those around us. Just as gold must be refined to achieve its most precious luster, all human beings must undergo a process of transformation that allows us to reach our maximum potential, reflecting the glory of our Creator.

The brilliance we exhibit is produced by God within us, illuminating a world that started well but is now lost and heading toward despair. In today's world, where everyone competes for their own ideals, it often seems that those who shine most publicly—regardless of whether they are genuinely the best—receive all the attention.

However, it is essential to understand that while shining is admirable, it is even more important to shine in the right way. This is particularly crucial if we wish to impact our children, our families, and those around us, as well as future generations, who will learn from what we pass on to them. If we conducted a survey asking hundreds of people whether they wish to shine or stand out in life, the vast majority, if not all, would likely say yes. In truth, we all desire to shine like gold and succeed in all areas of our lives.

If that were not the case, we would not feel the urge to be successful, to be admired, and to set an example for those who follow. The desire to shine is valid and beneficial, and it is something we should all cultivate in our lives; however, for many individuals, those desires often remain just that—"desires."

Dreaming While Awake

I believe that no one is born a failure or intended to be a loser. No one plans for their failures and defeats, regardless of how their life turns out. From a young age, we dream of a wonderful future; sometimes these dreams become so strong that others call us "dreamers." Personally, I used to enjoy daydreaming as a child. Despite growing up in a humble home, I loved to imagine a perfect world where I played an important role, where I had everything in abundance, and lacked nothing. Then, I would wake up to reality and find myself in the same place. But for those moments, I truly enjoyed it, and if given the chance, I would spend the whole daydreaming while awake.

This love for dreaming has helped me develop a positive attitude toward life's circumstances, always hoping that things will one day be different and that my dreams will come true. Even as an adult, I constantly seek ways to learn and improve myself, always aiming to develop the best version of my life. I am not in pursuit of riches or material possessions, nor do I seek recognition from others; I simply desire to shine more each day, reflecting the light of my Lord Jesus Christ and, ultimately, leave a legacy that my family will be proud of.

In short, I believe we all want to shine and have a better future, where our children remember us and can follow our example. However, for many, this dream becomes a nightmare that seems almost impossible to achieve. It can feel very challenging to reach this level of success, causing many to give up before reaching their goals. As I stated before, I firmly believe that instead of focusing on what is difficult and seemingly impossible, we should concentrate on our goals, knowing that we have the best example of persistence and resilience in Jesus, as shown throughout human history. If Jesus overcame, then we can too.

But how do we shine correctly?

While studying the gold refining process, I was fascinated by the information I gathered about this precious mineral that our planet produces. It's interesting to know that the purer one wants the gold to be, the longer the transformation process takes. The process requires persistence through long hours or days of treatments involving fire and chemicals. The more the gold is subjected to the challenges of large machinery and tools, the better the final product becomes. Ultimately, everything is worth it if one wishes to obtain the purest and most refined gold available on the market.

What I learned was both inspiring and enlightening, and I want to share it with you. Moreover, I want to illustrate how we can apply this transformation process to our own lives, especially in the current times we live in. I will reference some common terms used in the industrial gold refining process. This study aims to inspire you to move beyond the initial steps to achieve the goal of shining as brightly as God desires us to, reaching our fullest potential.

In What Stage Are We?

Let's examine what stage each of us is in: whether we have completed the refining process, are nearing completion, or are just beginning the transformation. Regardless of your current level, the most important thing is not to give up. Persevere until you achieve your goals; God is on your side and will never leave you. Before the foundation of the world, He had already chosen you, conceiving you in His mind and heart, and then using your family as the vehicle to bring you into this world.

The final results were already written from the beginning. God has a great conclusion in mind for your transformation process. Do not stop, even if the process sometimes hurts, bothers, wounds, or challenges you. The key is to maintain your faith, develop your ear to hear the voice of God, and, above all, allow yourself to be refined like gold so that you can then shine and display the beauty of God in your life.

Continue reading, and together we can find answers to the common question many of us ask at some point in our lives: Why can't I shine if I desire it so much and long to be the best version of myself?

CHAPTER 2

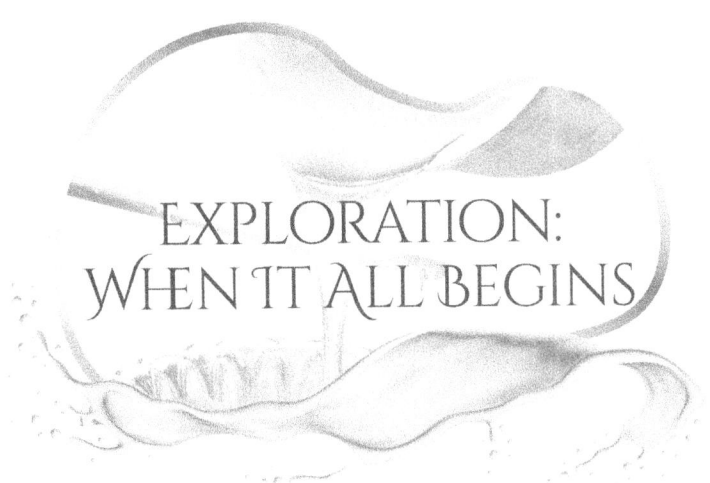

EXPLORATION: WHEN IT ALL BEGINS

When I studied the Word of God for the first time at the Bible Institute, I was fascinated by the construction of the golden lampstand (Menorah). This lampstand illuminated Israel's most important meeting place and was made of pure gold. It was a key piece in the Tabernacle, positioned in the Holy Place alongside other significant accessories. The Tabernacle was regarded as the most sacred meeting place where God descended to communicate with His people. Only the priests had access to the Holy Place, and the High Priest could enter the Most Holy Place only once a year. God provided specific instructions regarding the entire design of the Tabernacle. He detailed everything, from measurements and materials to fabrics, priestly garments, ornaments, and accessories. Even the priests' undergarments needed to be made of the material He commanded: fine linen. This highlights that God is a God of order, and when He communicates with us, He expects us to follow His instructions precisely. Specifically concerning the lampstand, God began by telling them:

> "Make a lampstand of pure gold. Its base and shaft are to be made of hammered work; its flowerlike cups, its buds and its blossoms shall be of one piece with it."
> Exodus 25:31

Indeed, I was fascinated when I read that the lampstand was made using hammered work, which symbolizes the journey of Christians coming to the feet of Christ. Through trials and challenges—what we often refer to as trials—our character is shaped. Just as gold begins to shine through this transformative process, so do we. Imagining the craftsmanship involved in hammering a piece of gold by hand, I realize it must have been no easy task. I picture the artisan striking the precious metal repeatedly to mold it into the unique and intricate form of a lampstand.

The amount of effort he must have invested is remarkable. It must have taken long hours of dedicated work to achieve such a feat, especially since there were no modern machines to ease the process; everything had to be done by hand. I can envision the great satisfaction the artist felt upon completing his creation, looking at the finished product with a smile on his face and joy in his eyes as he lit the first wick on the beautiful lampstand. We are not talking about a small lamp for a tabletop; this was a magnificent lampstand weighing 33 kilos, or approximately 73 pounds, far from the ones we typically use. I imagine that the gold appeared beautiful, shiny, strong, and perfect, but it wasn't always that way.

To achieve such a splendid result, the gold had to undergo a lengthy transformation process. It's worth noting that the gold commanded by God was of the highest quality, refined to near perfection. If the refining process for pure gold today is lengthy and meticulous, even with advanced technology, it must have been even more so in ancient times when everything was done manually. One can only speculate that if gold could speak, it might have resisted undergoing such an arduous procedure.

Exploration Stage

One of the first stages in gold mining is the exploration of the terrain, searching for signs of gold hidden deep within the earth. This exploration phase initiates a slow and thorough process of locating land that may contain valuable minerals, which can be mined at a reasonable cost. During this stage, deep drilling is conducted to take samples from various layers of soil to detect any presence of precious minerals, specifically gold. If gold is found, further deep drilling is carried out to extract samples from different depths to determine how much gold can be extracted, its type, and other important characteristics of the mineral.

However, it's important to note that when we see mountainous terrain, it often doesn't resemble a place where a gold mine might be hidden. In many cases, especially in desert areas, the initial exploration reveals only dry, barren land weathered by time and harsh conditions. The destructive climate and hurricane storms can leave behind a solitary and desolate landscape.

The exploration stage requires those searching for gold to believe and have faith that it exists, even when it is not visible. This is a stage of blind searching. In many locations, signs of gold can be identified by black earth or sand. This is a paradox: how can something so precious be found within something so dark and unattractive? The Bible states in 1 Corinthians 1:27-29:

> "But God has chosen the foolish things of the world to put to shame the wise, and God has chosen the weak things of the world to put to shame the things which are mighty; and the base things of the world and the things which are despised God has chosen, yes, and the things which are not,

to bring to nothing the things that are, that
no flesh should glory in His presence."

We can draw a parallel to our Christian lives: God similarly treats us. Many times, at first glance, people cannot see anything good in us. We are belittled and judged for our behavior, especially if we are assertive or do not conform to societal expectations. Yet, it is precisely from those who are perceived as the least that God aims to create the greatest.

If you are despised, rejoice, for you are chosen by God to humble the wise!

Although many may make us feel that we are alone, filled with hatred, resentment, and bitterness that darken our lives, I want to reassure you that God is in control, even when we cannot perceive His presence. This is especially difficult when life throws challenges our way, leading us to feel desolate and isolated. The harshness of our trials can leave our spirits devoid of life, leaving us in despair.

However, behind that façade of loneliness and sadness, behind the smile that disguises inner pain, and beneath the weight of darkness, lies a treasure of immense value waiting to be discovered. This is the raw gold that is destined to be refined. Then, it is when we allow God to work in us that He begins to reveal His love and mercy.

This marks the beginning of a transformative journey, where we start to allow our Refiner to explore us.

Often, we begin to seek our faith—a faith buried beneath the black sands of doubt—during moments of loneliness, need, or hopelessness. We may wish to be discovered by God, our Refiner, yet we hesitate to take that step of faith, often reluctant to surrender our pride, which serves no purpose.

We may not want to accept the reality that we will be tested by fire, as the prophet stated, and put through trials where the impurities that prevent us from seeing His glory will be revealed. Indeed, as we embark on this journey, we resemble uncharted lands where gold may lie beneath the surface. God already knows the potential He has placed within us and will begin to reveal it so that we can see how His power is perfected in our weaknesses. We are like earthen vessels, and our experiences serve to highlight God's glory rather than our own.

He Will Begin to Order Your Steps

As we begin to explore our lives and allow Him to guide us, He starts to order our steps. Before we can become that lampstand of pure gold, we must undergo a refining process. Once this process reaches its appropriate level, we will have the chance to become a beautiful instrument that illuminates, just as the lampstand does, crafted through the process of hammering.

Many of us, when we come to the feet of Christ and start studying or learning about the Holy Scriptures, know very little about the Word of God or the ordinances of our Lord. Some of us have such challenging character traits that only through the process of refining, like hammering, can we be transformed.

It is important to recognize that God always knew there was gold within you, even if you walked through life unaware of its existence. God seeks to uncover it. Open your heart so that He can begin this exploration process. Understand that it may be an intense journey, as He will address various aspects of your life. However, I assure you that it will be worth it. God desires even more than you do for you to allow yourself to be explored and to discover the potential you carry within. That potential was placed in you by God, your Creator, even before you were born.

CHAPTER 3

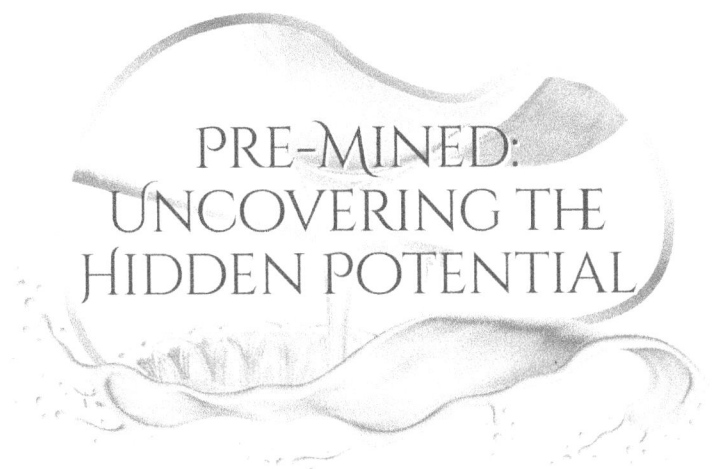

PRE-MINED: UNCOVERING THE HIDDEN POTENTIAL

The pre-mining process involves removing the top layer of organic soil to access the terrain beneath it for exploitation. In this discussion, we will concentrate on the initial stage of this process, where the "gold" (representing our potential) is concealed among the "rock" (symbolizing our imperfections). We will explore how God discovers us and recognizes our value, even when we fail to see it ourselves. Topics such as divine discovery, hidden potential, and inherent value will be addressed. Picture a mine—a deep, dark place where rock and earth hide precious treasures. This is how God perceives us: as mines filled with hidden potential, where the "gold" of our purpose and gifts awaits discovery.

In this chapter, we will delve into how God finds us within our personal "mine," revealing the inherent value that we often overlook. The mine represents our initial state, where our imperfections and limitations can obscure our true worth. Just as gold is hidden among stone, our divine potential lies beneath layers of insecurity, fear, or past experiences. Too often, we see ourselves as worthless "rock," failing to recognize the "gold" that God has placed within us.

Gold Never Runs Out

Let's talk about gold, the precious and highly coveted mineral that has adorned palaces, homes, temples, and shops across the world for centuries. While I'm not an expert, I've studied some interesting facts about gold. Have you ever wondered how gold is refined? Where is it found, or how does it seemingly never run out? Since ancient times, gold has been integral to our lives. Considered a precious gift from God, it shapes our cultures and the commerce industry.

Gold symbolizes purity, value, wealth, and durability; it's regarded as the finest of metals. Remarkably, gold does not tarnish, rust, or degrade over time. It maintains its worth, making it highly sought after by jewelers. The first mention of gold in the Bible is in Genesis when God speaks of the four rivers flowing from the Euphrates. He references the land of Havilah, stating,

> "The name of the first is Pishon; it winds through the entire land of Havilah, where there is gold. The gold of that land is good; aromatic resin and onyx are also there" (Genesis 2:11-12).

Here, gold is described as "good" or "fine," suggesting higher purity and value. Although it undergoes refining, fine gold is easier to work with. Gold has played a vital role throughout history, appearing in religious contexts, such as the construction of the Tabernacle and Solomon's Temple, where it was used extensively for utensils and furnishings. Additionally, gold was utilized in royal palaces and weaponry. Even today, gold remains relevant, continuously incorporated into evolving technologies. In essence, gold never goes out of style and retains its value.

Don't Rush—It's a Meticulous Process

If you're familiar with the gold refining process, you know it's meticulous and labor-intensive. If we attempted it, we might give up quickly! This can be likened to our spiritual lives: imagine if God gave up on us. Thankfully, He is patient, not wishing for anyone to perish but for all to come to repentance. Often, the lands that hide gold are not what we expect. Once it's discovered, a thorough cleaning of the terrain begins, removing everything that obstructs access to the gold.

The entire surface layer must be cleared, exposing only the area designated for extraction. Ironically, although gold is one of the most valuable metals, its initial appearance is far from appealing. Its beauty and quality are revealed through the refining process. When found in rivers, gold often appears as black dust mixed with sand and scrap metal.

This process mirrors our lives before coming to Christ. Many of us lived in sin and darkness, concealing our true selves with layers of masks. Once uncovered, we must submit to a transformative journey. Many may hesitate to follow through because the process can be challenging and daunting.

The refining of gold involves rigorous purification and separation using acids to eliminate impurities. Despite its high value, extracting gold remains difficult; in fact, about 80% of the world's gold has yet to be unearthed. Even with advanced technology, gold cannot be artificially produced—it is a natural mineral created by God, who ensures its exclusivity.

Inherent Value

God created us in His image, bestowing upon us inherent value that is independent of our abilities or achievements. Each person possesses unique gifts and talents—a "gold" that God desires to refine and utilize for His glory. As stated in 1 Corinthians 3:16,

> "Do you not know that you are the temple of God and that the Spirit of God dwells in you?"

When we compare our characteristics to those of gold, we may feel like we are nothing more than a thin layer of black dust, lacking the brilliance of gold and seemingly insignificant. However, in the eyes of our Creator, we are among the most important elements of His creation; we are His workmanship, made in His image and likeness, special treasures to Him.

Often, we feel unappreciated by others and believe they cannot see our potential, which can make us feel inferior. In reality, we are like unrefined gold that needs its layers removed. Many of us can relate to having a past filled with wounds, unforgiveness, bitterness, and depression.

Sometimes, we go through life recounting what others have done to us, often taking on the role of the victim because of the hurt we have experienced. What we tend to overlook is that those very layers—wounds, betrayals, rejections, and sufferings—are what polish our gold. As we heal and allow God to mend our wounds, it's as if the pre-mining process is stripping away the artificial layers that have hidden our true selves. These layers can cause so much damage, clouding our essence with bitterness and resentment, preventing us from shining.

Do You Know What Your War Trophy Is?

An important lesson is that what the enemy meant to destroy you, using diabolical instruments to entirely ruin you, God will turn to your favor and use it as a testimony. In other words, what the enemy intended for your end will become your weapon for a new beginning and your ultimate success. Start viewing yourself as a victorious man or woman, as a survivor of the enemy's attacks; this will become your war trophy. Let go of seeing yourself as a victim; it's time to rise as a warrior. Remember the sword David used to defeat Goliath? It was the same weapon that had once threatened and intimidated him.

During this process of healing, we can often find ourselves feeling overwhelmed, where everything makes us want to cry. But when the Holy Spirit begins to remove the layers that have blocked healing, we enter a beautiful stage of inner transformation. By giving the Holy Spirit, the freedom to enter and heal us, it's as if each superficial layer that robbed us of purity and shine is being exposed, allowing us to radiate the true quality of our gold. This is not a quick process; it depends on the extent of the damage beneath those layers. What's essential is that the exploration and pre-mining have begun. We know there is valuable gold beneath those layers; now it's time to start working on it.

Recognizing the Layers of "Rock"

It is crucial to identify the "rocks" that conceal our potential: fears, insecurities, and negative thought patterns. Reflect on past experiences that have shaped your self-perception. Once you uncover the hidden "gold," begin to explore your unique gifts and talents, identifying the areas where you feel passion and purpose. Seeking God's guidance through prayer and meditation on His Word is essential, allowing Him to reveal your true potential.

This understanding will help us embrace our divine value; in other words, to start seeing ourselves as God sees us and to accept that we are valuable in His eyes, imperfections and all. In doing so, we will cultivate a mindset of gratitude, acknowledging the gifts and talents that God has bestowed upon us.

> "For we are His workmanship, created in Christ Jesus for good works, which God prepared beforehand that we should walk in them." (Ephesians 2:10)

Our Own Personal Mine

Let's take a moment to reflect on our own personal "mine," identifying the "rocks" and seeking the hidden "gold." As we pray and meditate on the Word of God, we allow Him to reveal our potential, always remembering the importance of embracing the inherent value that He has given us. God sees us as mines filled with hidden potential. Through His love and grace, He invites us to explore our personal "mine," recognizing the value we may have forgotten and allowing Him to uncover the "gold" of our divine purpose.

If you feel that you are currently raw gold, with the process just beginning, that is perfectly fine. Don't give up, because the journey is worth it, and in the end, you will shine more brilliantly than you can imagine. Let us continue on the path toward total liberation, where the tears of the soul wash away the artificial layers that have previously submerged us in sorrow and bitterness. Allow the Holy Spirit to begin that beautiful work; cry if you need to but be sure to dry your tears and press on, as this is just the beginning.

CHAPTER 4

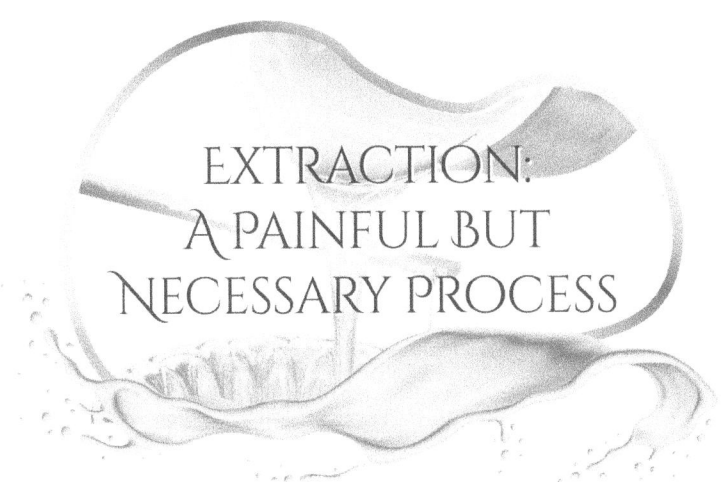

EXTRACTION: A PAINFUL BUT NECESSARY PROCESS

The gold refining process begins with mining, an essential stage where raw material containing gold, silver, and other minerals is extracted. Deep drilling is conducted, sometimes reaching depths of up to 3 kilometers, to access these hidden treasures. This mining process primarily focuses on drilling and exploiting the terrain. Let's explore the refining process and its spiritual parallel. Just as deep within our hearts and souls lie hidden aspects, we must bring them to light to uncover the layers of gold that have been buried over time. Many of us find it challenging to identify these aspects, but with God's help, we can achieve this. The key is to be honest and sincere with ourselves; if we are not, we are deceiving ourselves.

Now, let's discuss some rigorous steps in the gold refinement process that may seem unpleasant but are necessary.

Blasting: Revealing the Hidden

This stage involves careful drilling of the terrain, creating a network of holes filled with explosives. The controlled detonation of these explosives, known as blasting, fractures the rock and exposes the minerals to the surface. After blasting, loading, and hauling occur, the extracted material is removed, creating vast excavations called open pits. Large trucks and shovels then transport this material to leaching facilities, where the gold is recovered.

This physical process mirrors our spiritual journey. Just as miners extract minerals, the deepest wounds that separate us from God often lie hidden within our deepest selves. Discovering the hidden potential within our "mine" marks the beginning of a spiritual extraction process. In our innermost depths, the strongest wounds that keep us distant from God are concealed. Once we uncover this hidden potential, the extraction process can start. Similar to how miners excavate and separate precious minerals from rock, God guides us through challenges that may be painful but are essential for releasing the "gold" of our character.

Extraction:

A Process of Trials and Challenges

Extraction symbolizes the difficulties and trials we face in life. Just as the extraction of minerals requires effort and often involves difficult conditions, our spiritual growth can also be an arduous process. These trials can manifest in various ways, including health problems, financial difficulties, conflicts in relationships, or internal struggles with sin and doubt. Although we know that God is not the author of pain or suffering, we often wonder why He allows it.

The Bible teaches us that pain can have a redemptive purpose. God does not delight in seeing His children suffer; trials or obstacles in life can come from different sources. Yet, if God allows them, we must understand that through these trials, He molds and purifies us, eliminating the impurities that prevent us from growing in our faith.

> "And after you have suffered a little while, the God of all grace, who has called you to His eternal glory in Christ, will Himself restore, confirm, strengthen, and establish you." (1 Peter 5:10)

Jesus Himself was not exempt from trials and tribulations; on the contrary, He suffered even unto death on a cross, although He did not deserve it. Just as gold cannot be refined without being extracted from rock, our character cannot be transformed without facing challenges. Trials reveal our weaknesses and force us to depend on God, thereby strengthening our faith and our relationship with Him. Despite everything Jesus experienced, He relied on His Heavenly Father. He faced scorn, betrayal, slander, and even death on the cross; yet His communion with His Heavenly Father strengthened Him daily, filling Him with the grace needed not only to heal and perform miracles but also to endure the most difficult moments.

> "Not only so, but we also glory in our sufferings because we know that suffering produces perseverance; perseverance, character; and character, hope." (Romans 5:3-4)

It is crucial to understand that as we navigate the extraction process, we must find our strength in God. During trials, it is essential to seek His strength and comfort. Prayer, reading the Bible, and the support of the Christian community can help us overcome these challenges.

> "God is our refuge and strength, an ever-present help in trouble." (Psalm 46:1)

Learning from Trials

Every trial we face presents an opportunity for growth. We must seek God's wisdom to understand the purpose behind our suffering. Trials can teach us patience, humility, compassion, and dependence on God. It's also essential to recognize that we often label the consequences of our poor decisions as "trials." These are situations God warned us about, yet we didn't heed His advice because we wanted to follow our desires.

In such cases, we must acknowledge our mistakes and ask God for forgiveness, being attentive to the guidance of the Holy Spirit. We have all made mistakes; what matters is that we do not remain entrenched in them. Ignoring our wrongdoing can lead to disobedience and rebellion, resulting in curses and negative consequences that could have been avoided.

Therefore, it is often during our suffering that we must embrace the greater purpose behind it. While the pain is real, we can find hope in knowing that God has a plan for our suffering, regardless of any mistakes we may have made. Through our trials, God is preparing us for a greater purpose, using our experiences for His glory and to bless others. I encourage you, dear reader, to reflect on the trials and challenges you've faced throughout your life, particularly those you've encountered recently.

Seek God's strength and comfort during these difficult times. It is crucial to understand that while God does not bring about our trials, He allows them and often does so because we need to endure them to become better individuals. Trust in God's purpose, even amid suffering.

Lastly, remember that the refining process, though painful, is vital for revealing the "gold" of our character. Through our trials and challenges, God shapes and purifies us, preparing us to fulfill our divine purpose. Sometimes, this process means confronting difficult situations that expose our weaknesses and areas needing healing.

> "For you, O God, have tested us; you have refined us as silver is refined." (Psalm 66:10)

Unhealed wounds, resentment, and hidden sins can act as "rocks" that hinder our spiritual growth. Spiritual mining involves removing everything that prevents us from becoming the best version of ourselves, as God intended.

The Depth of the Wound

Often, the deepest wounds lie hidden beneath layers of denial, justification, or evasion. In His wisdom, God guides us through the "drilling" of these layers, allowing His light to reveal what has been concealed.

> "For the word of God is living and active, sharper than any double-edged sword, piercing to the division of soul and of spirit, of joints and of marrow, and discerning the thoughts and intentions of the heart." (Hebrews 4:12)

Each of us must recognize that going through a process of healing is often difficult. Drilling can be painful, as it requires us to confront our fears, insecurities, and sins. If we were told exactly when and what the next trial in our lives would entail, we would likely try to avoid it.

Nevertheless, this process is essential for our healing and liberation. We need to be "drilled" to be filled with the presence of God. Once the ground is drilled, God allows the "blasting" of His truth to expose the rocks of our hearts. This blasting can take the form of revelations, convictions, or confrontations that force us to face our realities.

"And you will know the truth, and the truth will set you free." (John 8:32)

Exposing Our Wounds to the Light of God

This is the only way to achieve liberation and transformation. By exposing our wounds to the light of God, we permit His grace to heal and transform us. While blasting can be dramatic, it leads to greater freedom and authenticity in our relationship with God. It is essential for everything that does not please Him to be cleared from our lives, allowing us to become like refined gold.

Beloved brothers, and sisters, I invite you to reflect on your wounds and areas of pain, not to feel sorry for your situation, but I encourage you to seek the guidance of the Holy Spirit during this process of spiritual "mining." Make prayer a disciplined part of your life by setting aside time each day to pray, meditate, and be in God's presence. It's crucial to live a life continuously seeking God's presence so that He may equip you for every good work.

As I mentioned before, in addition to prayer, confession, and the support of the Christian community are vital for achieving healing. Like the literal mining process, spiritual mining can also be challenging, but it is essential for our purification and growth in Christ. By allowing God to lead us into the depths of our being, we can experience the healing and liberation that only He can provide.

It is important to understand that God is a gentleman; He does not force anyone. He will knock on the door of your heart, but it is up to you to open it and remove the padlock that has rusted with time and painful memories.

When you open the door to Him, be sure to discard the padlock forever, allowing your heart to continually receive healing and enjoy His presence. God is the Master par excellence; He loves you and desires only the best for your life. If you let Him begin His work His way, I assure you that your life will never be the same, and you will see remarkable results.

CHAPTER 5

CRUSHING: BREAKING DOWN RESISTANCES

After extraction, the ore undergoes a crushing process in which the rock is broken into smaller pieces. This stage symbolizes the confrontation of our negative patterns and resistances, which is a crucial step on the path to purification and spiritual growth. In every Christian's life, we will encounter internal resistance for various reasons. We all have our experiences; thus, the crushing symbolizes the process of confronting and breaking these internal barriers that prevent us from growing. These resistances can manifest as negative thought patterns, harmful habits, ingrained fears, or stubborn attitudes. Just as a crusher breaks hard rock, God helps us confront and overcome these obstacles.

Identifying Negative Patterns

While it may not be easy, it is vital to identify the negative patterns that hinder our progress. These can include:

- Constant self-criticism

- Fear of failure

- A tendency to procrastinate

- The need for control

- Resentment and bitterness

- And many more...

The Word of God and the guidance of the Holy Spirit can help us discern these patterns. Although confronting our negative patterns can be uncomfortable and painful, it is absolutely necessary for achieving permanent results; therefore, it is essential for our liberation and transformation. As stated in Hebrews 12:1

> "Therefore, since we are surrounded by such a great cloud of witnesses, let us throw off everything that hinders us and the sin that so easily entangles, and let us run with perseverance the race marked out for us."

However, the process of liberation and change requires surrender and humility. In order to break our resistances, we must submit to God's will and acknowledge our need for His help. Humility allows us to recognize our weaknesses and accept change. Additionally, transformation begins with the renewal of our minds. We must replace negative thought patterns with the truth of God's Word.

Romans 12:2 reminds us,

> "Do not conform to the pattern of this world but be transformed by the renewing of your mind. Then you will be able to test and approve what God's will is—his good, pleasing and perfect will."

Therefore, we have the Holy Spirit, our greatest ally, by our side. Jesus promised He would send the Holy Spirit to guide us into all truth and righteousness. The Holy Spirit empowers us to conquer our resistances and experience liberation. He guides us, strengthens us, and helps us develop new patterns of thought and behavior.

Let us take time to reflect on our negative patterns and resistances. We should seek God's guidance through prayer and meditation on His Word. It's crucial to remember the importance of surrender, humility, and the renewal of the mind. This chapter teaches us that while being crushed can be challenging, it is an essential step on our path to transformation.

By confronting and breaking down our internal resistances, we allow God to shape us into His image and prepare us for His purpose. This process will not be easy, as we must recognize that we too have hurt others, whether through our words, looks, attitudes, comments, or other means. Additionally, it is important that when we wrong someone, we are prepared to ask for forgiveness and admit our imperfections. As Scripture reminds us in James 3:2,

> "For we all stumble in many ways. If anyone does not stumble in what he says, he is a perfect man, able also to bridle his whole body."

God is not seeking perfect individuals but rather those who, despite their imperfections, have hearts willing to be molded, crushed, refined, and transformed by the power of His glory to demonstrate the brilliance of His presence.

CHAPTER 6

THE CRUCIBLE: THE PURIFYING FIRE OF TRANSFORMATION

Introducing the ore into a crucible, where it undergoes high temperatures, serves to melt the gold and separate impurities. This stage symbolizes the divine transformation in our lives, where we are refined through intense challenges, allowing the "gold" of our character to shine more clearly. The crucible is a powerful metaphor in the Bible, representing the painful yet essential journey of purification and transformation that God uses. Through trials and tribulations, we are refined like gold, free from impurities and prepared to fulfill our divine purpose. While it may not sound encouraging, we can see that the challenges we face serve to purify us, cleanse us, and help us improve each day.

As we endure the crucible, we become fortified, positioned to bless others. I'm not sure if you've ever seen a crucible. It resembles a cauldron, but it is much stronger and can withstand high temperatures, making it ideal for melting gold. Unlike a regular cauldron, which would not endure the intense heat, or the long duration required, a crucible excels in this function. When the gold reaches the point of transformation, it undergoes a painful process: it melts at around 1,064.43 degrees Celsius (1,947.97 degrees Fahrenheit).

The gold remains in the crucible for hours, enduring the heat until it is refined and purged of all its impurities. Following this, it is washed with cold water. This step is essential; there is no alternative. The gold must be melted to purify it; the impurities need to be separated from what is precious.

If that gold could speak, I'm sure it would never willingly endure this process.

When we draw a parallel to our own lives, we find that there are moments when our problems can feel overwhelming, almost as if they are melting us down. Often, even if we don't fully understand it, God allows these trials because they are sometimes the only way to capture our attention. How many times have we felt exhausted, believing we can't endure anymore?

We question how what we are experiencing can align with God's promises. God assures us of blessings, yet we face trials. He promises us peace, yet we feel the chaos of daily struggles. God speaks of prosperity, but debts seem unending. The enemy often uses these circumstances to dim our light, preventing us from shining.

Painful but Necessary Process

Importantly, God does not leave us alone during these trials. He is with us at all times; although we may go through the crucible, the Holy Spirit always comes to refresh us. Once the Holy Spirit arrives and rejuvenates us, we will be ready to continue shining. After being refined, we can see how we increasingly radiate as the Lord strengthens us. Therefore, if you are currently experiencing a refining process and feeling the heat of the flames, do not give up. As stated in Malachi 3:3,

> "He will sit as a refiner and purifier of silver; he will purify the Levites and refine them like gold and silver. Then the LORD's offerings will be brought in righteousness."

Remember, gold must be subjected to fire to be purified, and once refined, it shines beautifully. After you are refined like gold, your offering to God will be greatly improved. Do not shy away from the crucible. Avoid complaining each time a challenge arises in your life; do not adopt a victim mentality. Instead, learn to worship God amidst your trials; this will serve as a soothing balm in times of pain. Cultivate an attitude of gratitude even for the negative experiences, drawing lessons from them. As Romans 8:28 reminds us:

> "And we know that in all things God works for the good of those who love him, who have been called according to his purpose."

One aspect I found compelling while studying the refining of gold is that "gold cannot be mixed with anything but itself." The crucible symbolizes the intense trials and challenges we face, which can feel like a scorching fire. Just as gold is melted at high temperatures to remove impurities, God allows us to undergo "fire" through trials for our purification. While this process can be painful, it is vital for our transformation and spiritual growth.

We should understand that God does not permit suffering out of cruelty, but rather out of love. He wants to free us from the impurities that keep us from living fully in His grace. Through the crucible, we are molded into the image of Christ, developing stronger character and deeper faith. Zechariah 13:9 says:

> "And I will bring the third part through the fire, and will refine them as silver is refined,

> and will try them as gold is tried. They shall call on my name, and I will hear them: I will say, It is my people: and they shall say, The LORD is my God."

Trials can reveal our weaknesses and bring our hidden impurities to light. By facing these challenges with God's help, we can experience profound transformation in our character and our relationship with Him. It is through these trials that our character is tested, and our faith is strengthened. While we are going through the process of transformation, it's crucial to develop trust in the one who created the purifying fire; this fire is not meant to destroy you, but to refine you. During trials, it's essential to believe in God's purifying purpose. Remember, God is present in the midst of the fire, sustaining and strengthening you. Isaiah 43:2 assures us:

> "When you pass through the waters, I will be with you; and when you pass through the rivers, they will not sweep over you. When you walk through the fire, you will not be burned; the flames will not set you ablaze."

As we learn from the fire of trials, let's acknowledge that these experiences can teach us valuable lessons about patience, humility, and dependence on God.

We should seek God's wisdom to understand our suffering's purpose and grow through it. As we navigate the challenging process of refinement, we will emerge from the crucible like refined gold, possessing a purer character and a stronger faith. Our experiences can serve as powerful testimonies to God's grace and transformative power.

When gold is melted, it experiences boiling at high temperatures, causing any dross, residue, or impurities to rise to the surface due to the pressure generated by the intense heat. This pressure, at its peak, effectively removes the impurities that accumulate in the mixture. Similarly, the all-consuming fire can bring out our best essence, helping us separate the dross—those negative aspects in our attitudes and behaviors.

Fire and Water: Two Stages of Transformation

Therefore, I invite you to reflect on the intense trials you have faced. I encourage you to trust in God's purifying purpose during difficult times. Remember the importance of learning from these trials and allowing God to transform us. This chapter reminds us that while the crucible may be painful, it is an essential process for our transformation. Through the "fire" of trials, God purifies and molds us into His image, preparing us to reflect His glory. As we endure the crucible, we are shaped into the likeness of Christ, developing a stronger character and deeper faith.

Purification is necessary for a closer relationship with God.

However, there is good news: amid the trials of fire, there are also moments of refreshment. Fire and water are both crucial to the transformation process. The water of the Holy Spirit is poured into our lives, renewing our spirits. Not every moment is filled with pain or suffering; there will be times of inspiration and motivation from the Holy Spirit, encouraging us not to give up and to keep moving forward.

Going through the crucible is indeed painful, but it is a necessary purification process for each of us. Just as gold must endure high temperatures to remove impurities, we too face trials allowed by God for our purification. God does not bring suffering out of cruelty; rather, He is love. He desires to free us from the burdens of sin, resentment, and pride that hinder us from living fully in His grace. Though this process can be challenging and painful, it is essential for our spiritual growth. As stated in Psalm 66:10,

> "For you, O God, have tested us; you have refined us as silver is refined."

The Fire of the Crucible

Trials and tribulations can feel like a scorching fire, revealing our weaknesses and purifying our hearts.

However, during this time, God is present, sustaining and strengthening us to endure the process, while the water of His Spirit is poured out upon us. Following the fire, God refreshes us with the "water" of the Holy Spirit, healing our wounds and renewing our strength. The Holy Spirit comforts, guides, and empowers us to shine with the light of Christ. He is the one who helps us recover and move forward.

By cultivating an intimate relationship with the Holy Spirit, you will gain insights that may otherwise be difficult to understand from God's perspective. The Holy Spirit is your Comforter; He strengthens, guides, and equips you for every good work. Trust in Him and strive to know Him more each day; He desires communion with you.

Transformation into a Testimony

The time to shine has arrived; all the suffering, trials, and difficult experiences can become blessings and serve as a testimony to the grace, mercy, and goodness of God. After enduring the crucible, we are transformed into living testimonies of God's grace and power. Our experiences can inspire and encourage others who are facing similar challenges. When we emerge victorious from our trials, we can offer support to those navigating similar situations. Our lives, refined by fire and refreshed by water, become valuable offerings to God. The faith we strengthen through our trials enables us to serve God and others more effectively.

So, dear reader, I encourage you to trust in God's purification process, even amid pain. Remember to seek the comfort and guidance of the Holy Spirit during your trials. Most importantly, begin to share your testimony of transformation so that others may find hope in God. Remember that the crucible symbolizes God's transforming love and grace. Through trials, we are refined and purified, emerging as shining testimonies of His power and faithfulness.

CHAPTER 7

LEACHING: THE DEEP PURIFICATION OF THE SOUL

In this chapter, we explore the processes of leaching, washing, and chemical mixtures as metaphors for the deep purification of the soul. Just as these processes separate precious metals from impurities, God employs similar methods to cleanse and refine us. Leaching, the process in which hidden impurities are extracted through a liquid, mirrors how God exposes and eliminates the hidden flaws in our hearts. This process may involve confronting sins, unhealed wounds, or negative thought patterns that hinder our spiritual growth. Just as a liquid dissolves and removes impurities from ore, the Word of God and the Holy Spirit reveal and eliminate the impurities from our souls.

> "For the word of God is living and active, sharper than any double-edged sword, piercing to the division of soul and spirit, of joints and marrow, and discerning the thoughts and intentions of the heart." (Hebrews 4:12)

Through His grace, God guides us in this extraction process, helping us identify and release the burdens that inhibit us from living fully in His love. This journey may involve confession, repentance, and seeking healing through prayer and the Christian community. Washing, a process of deep cleansing, symbolizes how God purifies us from the stain of sin and renews us through His grace. Just as water cleanses dirt, the blood of Christ washes us and transforms us into new creations. This process helps us feel renewed and clean, enabling a deeper relationship with our Father.

Cleansing Through Grace

It is essential to understand that, as Christians, redeemed by the blood of Christ who died for us and for all of humanity's sins, spiritual cleansing is not achieved through our own efforts but by the grace of God. His grace forgives, heals, and empowers us to live lives free from the impurities of our past.

> "If we confess our sins, he is faithful and just to forgive us our sins and to cleanse us from all unrighteousness." (1 John 1:9)

In other words, it is by His grace and love that the Holy Spirit renews us. When the Holy Spirit transforms our hearts and minds, He guides us into truth, strengthens us in the fight against sin, and helps us develop a character similar to that of Christ. The Holy Spirit enables us to be completely renewed and fosters a closer relationship with God.

The Power of Forgiveness

God forgives us, blotting out our sins and freeing us from guilt and condemnation. This forgiveness allows us to experience the freedom and peace that only God can give. Forgiveness is a process that liberates us and helps us move forward without the burdens of the past. Therefore, I invite you to seek God's deep cleansing through confession and repentance, and to receive God's grace and forgiveness, allowing Him to heal the wounds of the past.

Never forget the importance of renewal by the Holy Spirit, allowing Him to transform our heart and mind because the Holy Spirit is kind and a complete gentleman; He will not force anything in your life, but will work within you according to how you allow Him. This chapter reminds us that leaching and washing symbolize the deep cleansing of the soul. Through

God's grace and forgiveness, we are purified and renewed, allowing us to reflect His image more clearly.

Cleansing and Purifying the Soul

Washing, a process of deep cleansing, represents how God purifies us from the stain of sin and renews us with His grace. Just as water cleanses dirt, the blood of Christ washes us and makes us new creatures. Now, it is very important to understand that grace does not mean that we are constantly sinning against Him and then humbling ourselves to receive His forgiveness. It's not that you will be perfect, but you do need to be careful not to offend God's heart and grieve the Holy Spirit, because He will depart if you do not obey Him and do not take care of your relationship with Him. Remember that we said He is a gentleman and does not force anyone; He also does not stay when you remove Him from your life by prioritizing sin and disobeying Him.

> "If we confess our sins, he is faithful and just to forgive us our sins and to cleanse us from all unrighteousness." (1 John 1:9)

Here we can experience God's purifying action when, in His mercy, He washes us with His love and renews us with His Holy Spirit, allowing us to start anew and walk in His light. Water represents the word of God, which cleanses and sanctifies us. Something very important is that if only some ingredients are used to soften the process, then it will not work. In the same way, we need God's grace and mercy in our lives, but you also have a responsibility in the process, which is to be sensitive to God's voice when He speaks to you, to have an attitude of submission to His perfect will, and to love Him with all your heart, mind, soul, and body. When we love Him, the process is more bearable, because the love for His presence will make you obey Him in everything He tells you, even if you do not understand it at the moment, as Jesus said to Peter, "What you do not understand now you will understand later."

Chemical Mixtures: Complete Transformation

Then comes a process of chemical mixtures that will serve to continue the cleansing and refining process. Chemical mixtures, the combination of substances to create a new solution, represent how God completely transforms us, molding us into the image of Christ. In our Christian life, we can apply this concept when, through the combination of His Word, His Spirit, and our experiences, God creates a new person in us, free from the impurities of the past. Usually, it is not something that arises overnight but a slow process where God transforms, cleanses, heals, and restores according to how we allow Him. Of one thing we are sure, and that is that we are going through the process of transformation.

> "Therefore, if anyone is in Christ, the new creation has come: The old has gone, the new is here!" (2 Corinthians 5:17)

God, in His wisdom, uses various "mixtures" of circumstances and experiences to refine us and prepare us for His purpose. Just as chemicals combine to create a purer solution, God combines His grace and our faith to produce a complete transformation. Therefore, my beloved reader, I encourage you to seek God's deep purification, allowing Him to expose and eliminate the impurities of your soul. Remember the importance of confession, repentance, and seeking healing through prayer and the Christian community. The Word of God tells us,

> "Confess your sins to each other and pray for each other so that you may be healed" (James 5:16).

Therefore, it is important to find someone to accompany you in this process, if possible. Be sure to choose someone who is grounded in the Word of God, submitted to His authority, and a person of prayer who can help you break those chains in the spiritual realm so that you can receive your liberation.

Trust in God's transformation process, knowing that He is molding us into the image of Christ. Remember that leaching, washing, and chemical mixtures serve as powerful metaphors for the deep purification God performs in our lives. Through these processes, we are cleansed, renewed, and transformed, emerging as shining testimonies of His grace and love.

CHAPTER 8

YOUR REFINER

Let's begin this chapter by emphasizing that in order to reach the presence of God, you must open your heart to Him as your one and only Savior, if you haven't done so already. At this moment, allow me to introduce you to your Refiner; Jesus Christ, the one who will refine you like gold through an intimate relationship with you. He will purify you, cleanse you, separate you, and even crush you if necessary, but in the end, He will make you shine like you have never imagined. Today, He invites you to buy from Him gold refined by fire, eye salve for your spiritual vision, and white garments to cover your spiritual nakedness. Trust your Refiner, for even though you may pass through the fire, He will always be with you, just as He was with Daniel's friends in the fiery furnace, protecting them. Likewise, He has promised to be with you every day of your life.

> "I counsel you to buy from me gold refined in the fire, so you can become rich; and white robes to wear, so you can cover your shameful nakedness; and salve to put on your eyes, so you can see." (Revelation 3:18)

Never think that everything that happens or will happen in your life is meaningless or without purpose. God has already crafted a plan for your life, and He knows what is best for you. When you make wrong decisions, God does not discard you; however, the consequences are a natural result of your choices. If you sin, He may discipline you, and although this is often uncomfortable, it is necessary for your good. While God allows us to enter the furnace of affliction and be refined like gold in a crucible, He has promised to be with us always.

Many times, we find ourselves in situations we have created. God never desires our harm; He always seeks our success and triumph in life, especially to give Him glory. However, it is important to understand that God is not the author of death or suffering; but, He allows us to experience consequences that follow our misguided decisions so that we may learn from them.

Embarrassed to Admit

Have you ever found yourself in a position where you knew deep down that what was happening to you was your own fault due to foolish choices? Sometimes we disguise and deny this truth until the very end, embarrassed to admit and say, "I was wrong." I want you to know that God is our Refiner; He knows our worth and that from hard rock, black sand, and dirty yellow mud, something precious and bright can emerge—pure, refined gold, destined for high places, palaces, and seats among kings and priests, seated in heavenly places with Christ Jesus.

God specializes in transforming broken hearts; He heals and refines them. He can bring forth something beautiful and of great value from the most despised and lowly. God continually performs these transformations, even when we do not deserve them. This is precisely why He gave His only begotten Son so that we might be saved. You are chosen by God; you only need to believe it and embrace His precious promises.

God did not create you to live in depression, loneliness, misery, or unhappiness. Regardless of our humble beginnings or the wealth of others, we are the finest creation that God has made. If you are still uncertain about what God desires from you or how to seek Him, I challenge you today: believe in everything He has declared about you. Seek Him in spirit and truth, surrender completely, become obsessed with His presence, and fall in love with His goodness and mercy.

The Intentions of Our Hearts

He is the Alpha and the Omega, the beginning and the end, the Almighty God who knows all, searches all, and sees all. Before Him, we are fully exposed; we cannot hide our true selves, our thoughts, or the intentions of our hearts. In His presence, we are filled with His mercy. When He looks at us, He sees us as refined and perfected gold, gazing at us as the finished product. It does not matter who you are or how many flaws you possess. It does not matter how many times you have tried and failed; God sees you as the creation He has formed with His own hands.

God loves you and desires that you love Him in return; He longs for a relationship with you. When you feel most alone, remember that He is always willing to listen—just talk to Him. If you're feeling depressed, He is there to comfort you. When you're on the brink of temptation, cry out to Him, and He will help you find the strength to resist.

When you feel like you can't go on, He is there to give you the life and energy you need. Trust in Him, and you will see that He will never leave you, as He has promised. Don't you believe that if your life weren't important to Him, Jesus would not have died on the cross of Calvary? He did this out of love for you because

He cares deeply for you. I share this message with you in hopes that God will touch your heart through it.

Letter from God, Your Heavenly Father

January 14, 1998

Dear Child, how are you?

Please take a moment to listen, as I have something important to share with you. A long time ago, I faced a significant decision—one that was extremely difficult for me but essential for you. I saw you walking aimlessly and feeling distressed, knowing that this was not my plan for your life. I spoke earnestly with my only Son and asked Him if He would be willing to allow me to sacrifice Him so that you, my creation and adopted child, could one day be with me.

My only Son understood my pain in seeing you in that condition and accepted my proposal. He came to Earth, was born, and grew to be a good man. I blessed Him, and He helped many people. However, humanity mistreated Him; they slapped Him, spat in His face, and ultimately killed Him. I suffered greatly as I witnessed what they did to my beloved Son. It would have been easy for me to tell Him, "Forget it, my Son; do not suffer, and come back to me," but I could not, because you were at stake.

You are so important to me that I endured seeing my Son broken and suffering until His last breath on that cross. Yet, in dying, He fulfilled what was planned—this is Jesus, my beloved Son, who obeyed my command. Because he fulfilled His purpose and obeyed, you now have the opportunity to be with me. If you allow me to enter your heart, I will be with you forever, and I will never, ever leave you.

With much love,

Your Heavenly Father

Written by Edna L. Isaac, 1/14/98

In the Bible, we find a true story that took place many years ago, marking the history of a man who lost absolutely everything, yet God restored him with double blessings. God Himself declared Job to be a righteous man, stating that there was no one like him. This illustrates that even righteous, good, or morally decent people can endure moments of tragedy and trials.

The enemy attacked Job with relentless force, leaving him in ruin: he lost all his children, his health, and his wealth. Job was the richest man of his time; God had blessed him so abundantly that he lacked nothing until the enemy devastated him. While God could have intervened to prevent Job from experiencing such calamity, He allowed it to happen.

Job maintained that he had not faltered in God's eyes. I cannot cover all the details of Job's life here, but I highly recommend reading the entire book of Job. It is a fascinating story filled with profound mysteries. What I want to emphasize is that Job was a servant of God who had to endure significant trials before emerging victorious, shining even more brightly once his ordeal was over. God greatly rewarded him, restoring his fortunes and blessing him with daughters, the most beautiful women in that time, known for their beauty, and making him again the wealthiest man in the world. Here is a portion of Scripture from Job 22:22-26:

> Accept instruction from his mouth and lay up his words in your heart. If you return to the Almighty, you will be restored: If you remove wickedness far from your tent and assign your nuggets to the dust, your gold of Ophir to the rocks in the ravines, then the Almighty will be your gold, the choicest silver for you. Surely then you will find delight in the Almighty and will lift up your face to God.

Dear reader, I invite you to say this simple prayer, opening your heart to Jesus Christ.

Heavenly Father, I come before your presence humbled and asking for forgiveness for all my sins. I accept the sacrifice that Jesus made on the cross of Calvary. Write my name in the Book of Life and cleanse me with your precious blood. Holy Spirit, enter my heart and purify it. In Jesus' name, Amen.

If you have said this simple prayer, visit a church where the full gospel is preached and be persistent in your service to God. Welcome to the family of Christ Jesus!

CHAPTER 9

PURE REFINED GOLD: DISPLAYING ITS GLORY

The process of smelting gold is truly fascinating, involving many long hours of tedious and often dangerous work to achieve the refined gold that we desire. When we finally see the result, we can confidently say, "It was worth it." While different mines may use slightly varying methods, the result is almost pure gold, a metal that is highly valued and appreciated. I am particularly impressed by the strong chemicals that gold must endure and the intense heat it is subjected to in order to achieve its shine. During the separation of metals and other impurities, the smelter must continue the process until he can see the reflection of his face in the boiling gold. The fire does not burn the gold; instead, it purifies it. This remarkable process enhances the quality of the precious mineral, perfecting it and revealing its purest essence.

One description of the refining process explains that the solution rich in gold and silver is filtered and cleaned. First, oxygen is removed, and zinc powder is added to precipitate the metals and solidify them. The product of the Merrill-Crowe process then proceeds to the refining stage. The leftover solution, which contains no gold, is referred to as "barren." Nitric acid is used to attack copper and silver, and this process lasts between 6 to 12 hours.

Once the material is dissolved, it transitions from a metallic state to a liquid one. Upon completion of this stage, the result is a brown, oxidized liquid. Urea is introduced to neutralize the solution before gold is separated. Once neutralized, the liquid undergoes gassing with sulfur dioxide in the "pregnant solution" (a solution rich in gold). As the gas enters, the gold precipitates and settles at the bottom of the tank.

Once all the gold has fallen, what remains is a solution of copper and silver, which is transferred to another tank. The residue in the original tank, which resembles "yellow mud," is actually gold. At this point, the gold is 99% pure but requires washing with sulfuric acid to eliminate any remaining silver and copper.

Afterward, deionized water is used to wash the material through a sophisticated filtration system. The final product is gold powder, which is melted at a temperature of 2,200 degrees Fahrenheit (approximately 1,204 degrees Celsius) and cast into bars. It's incredible to consider all the steps gold must go through before it reaches the market.

Not Everyone Would Understand

Wow! It's incredible to consider all the stages and processes that occur before gold is refined. If we compare this to our spiritual lives, we can see that often, when we come to the feet of Christ, we experience a separation not only from the world of sin but also from people we once regarded as family. When we no longer engage in the same behaviors they do, they may turn their backs on us, stop inviting us, give us the cold shoulder—something we say in Puerto Rico—and even despise us.

Many times, this leads to feelings of loneliness, as if we have become completely separated from everyone. Some may find this isolation difficult to bear and choose to return to their old ways to please their family, thereby offending God's heart while seeking to keep their loved ones close. The process of separation is not easy. Yet, it is necessary to rid our lives of impurities, even if many will struggle to understand us. If we remain persistent, they will eventually witness the transformative power in our lives, and probably many of them will end up wanting or desiring what we have.

Are You Ready to Shine?

After the processes of leaching and washing, the gold has been purified and is ready to shine in its full splendor. This is the ultimate result of refinement: through transformation, we reflect the glory of God. Pure and bright gold symbolizes our character once it has been transformed, free of impurities and ready to reflect the light of Christ. Just as gold reflects light, we also, through refinement, reflect God's glory to the world.

This reflection is not about our glory; it is about the glory of God shining through us, demonstrating the reflection of Christ. As we are conformed to the image of Christ, we become mirrors of His love, grace, and truth. Our refined character serves as a living testimony to God's transformative power.

> "And we all, who with unveiled faces contemplate the Lord's glory, are being transformed into his image with ever-increasing glory, which comes from the Lord, who is the Spirit." (2 Corinthians 3:18)

Refinement prepares us to fulfill the purpose God has for us. Our transformed lives become powerful tools in God's hands to bless others and glorify His name. It is through this transformation that we begin to live in the glory of God, continuously experiencing His presence and developing an intimate relationship with Him through the Holy Spirit.

After refinement, we are called to walk in the light of Christ, living lives that honor His name. This means staying away from the impurities of the world and seeking holiness in all areas of our lives. Our light is meant to be shared with the world. We must witness God's grace and love, bringing hope and healing to those around us. In everything we do, we should give glory to God, recognizing Him as the source of our transformation and our shining.

Let us remember that our beautiful shine is not our own; it is the reflection of Christ in us. Just as the moon does not shine by itself but reflects the sun, we cannot shine through our own merits, but only through those of our Lord Jesus Christ, for He alone deserves all glory and honor forever and ever.

> "In the same way, let your light shine before others, that they may see your good deeds and glorify your Father in heaven." (Matthew 5:16)

Sharing the Wealth of Transformation

Once we have been refined and molded, we become a treasure in God's hands, ready to share the wealth of our transformation with others. In this way, we can use our experiences to bless those around us and glorify God. Our journey of transformation is a valuable treasure that we can share. Our testimony can inspire hope and encourage those who are going through similar trials. By sharing our personal experiences of God's transformative power, we can have a profound impact on the lives of others. Our stories can bring light and hope to a dark world.

Impact on the World

God calls us to serve others by using our gifts and talents to bless those around us. Through our service, we can reflect the love of Christ and bring healing and restoration. Our transformation can significantly impact the world, bringing hope and change to our communities. By living a life that honors God, we can be a bright light in a dark world.

We are called to be a blessing to others, sharing the grace and love we have received. Through serving others, we experience the fullness of God's purpose in our lives. In all that we do, we must give glory to God, recognizing that He is the source of our transformation and our impact on the world.

CONCLUSION

WHEN WE SHINE: TO HIM ALONE BE THE GLORY

We have journeyed together, exploring the profound meaning of spiritual refinement. Now, we face a crucial question: Are we truly willing to allow God to refine us so that we may reflect His glory? This is not a question to be taken lightly—it is an invitation to sincere introspection. The refining process is not an easy path; it involves confronting our impurities, weaknesses, and deepest fears. However, as we have seen, it is a necessary process to reveal the "gold" that God has deposited within us. Let us remember the words of Matthew 11:29-30:

> "Take my yoke upon you and learn from me, for I am gentle and humble in heart, and you will find rest for your souls. For my yoke is easy and my burden is light."

Through Christ, we find the strength and grace to endure the refining process. This process requires patience, perseverance, endurance, and dedication. It is not about competition or seeking the approval of others but about allowing God's light to shine through us. As Philippians 4:13 reminds us:

> "I can do all things through Christ who strengthens me."

What stage is your life right now?

Therefore, it is essential to remember that glory belongs solely to God. We must not seek to appropriate it; instead, we should recognize that we are simply vessels through which His light shines. Now, I invite you to reflect: In what stage of refinement do you find yourself? What lessons have you learned from the trials you have faced?

Every experience and every challenge has a divine purpose. Do not allow these moments to go to waste. If you have not yet begun the refining process, I encourage you to surrender to God's will.

Obedience, although sometimes difficult, is the path to transformation. By yielding to His purpose, you will discover that even amid trials, you can experience His peace and joy. Allow God to refine you, transform you, and make you shine with His glory. The world needs to see His light reflected in you. Refined gold is soft and malleable; it is free from corrosion and other substances. When gold is mixed with other metals, such as copper, iron, or nickel, it becomes harder, less malleable, and more corrosion resistant. This mixture is called an "alloy."

The higher the percentage of foreign metals, the harder the gold; conversely, the lower the percentage of alloy, the softer and more malleable the gold. What can this represent in our lives? The more contaminated we are with sin, offenses, and wounds, the harder we become. However, when we allow the Holy Spirit to work in us, we become more moldable. A pure heart is like pure gold—soft, malleable, and manageable. In contrast, an impure heart is like a hard rock. In other words, a pure heart allows itself to be molded by God.

Malleability: Being Molded for His Purpose

After being melted and purified, gold becomes malleable, allowing it to be shaped as desired. Similarly, through our own refinement, we become malleable in God's hands, ready to be molded for His purpose. The malleability of gold represents our willingness to be shaped by God. Just as gold submits to the craftsman, we too must submit to God's will, allowing Him to shape us according to His desires.

Each of us has a unique purpose, and God molds us to fulfill that purpose. Through trials and refinement, He prepares us to be used in His work. To be malleable means surrendering our will to God's will, trusting His wisdom and perfect plan.

> "For we are God's handiwork, created in Christ Jesus to do good works, which God prepared in advance for us to do." (Ephesians 2:10)

The Process of Being Molded

To be molded by God, we must surrender to His authority and obey His commands. Living a life of surrender and obedience involves trusting Him, even when we do not understand His ways. Our life is a continual journey of learning and growth. God molds us through various experiences, teaching us valuable lessons and helping us develop our character.

We must remain open to learning from each situation and allow God to transform us. As we are molded by God, we become more effective in His service, fulfilling our purpose in the world. Hebrews 3:13 warns that hearts can become hardened by the deceitfulness of sin. Failing to forgive produces bitterness, anger, and resentment.

> "See, I have refined you, though not as silver; I have tested you in the furnace of affliction." (Isaiah 48:10)

"In all this you greatly rejoice, though now for a little while you may have had to suffer grief in all kinds of trials. These have come so that the proven genuineness of your faith—of greater worth than gold, which perishes even though refined by fire—may result in praise, glory, and honor when Jesus Christ is revealed." (1 Peter 1:6-7)

ABOUT THE AUTHOR

Edna Isaac was born in the picturesque city of Aguadilla, Puerto Rico. Growing up in a humble home, her parents instilled in her the fundamental values that shape her identity today. Through her written words, Edna has become a voice of hope and transformation. Her deep connection to her Puerto Rican heritage is intertwined with her strong 34-year marriage to Francisco Isaac, also a native of the island. Together, they have the joy of raising their four beloved children: Charaliz, Krystaliz, Angeliz, and Nathiel Isaac.

A passion for writing has been a constant in Edna's life. Her literary journey began in the 1990s with the publication of her first book of poems. After publishing two more works, her entrepreneurial spirit led her to establish her own publishing house, JDN Publications. Through this platform, Edna has not only brought her own stories to life but has also dedicated herself to helping new authors realize their literary dreams, even extending support to those with limited resources in other countries.

With a career that includes over 13 authored literary works and two co-authored titles, Edna has developed a clear purpose in her writing: to be a beacon of hope for diverse populations facing suffering and significant challenges. A notable example of her impact is her book "El Silencio No Funciona" (Silence Doesn't Work), which has become a powerful support for campaigns against domestic violence.

Her innovative vision also led her to create a line of educational books under the EDUCATE Publishing imprint, launched through JDN Publications. This initiative birthed the brand "Challenging My Ego," which focuses on emotional intelligence, recognizing its vital importance in children's development.

With profound social sensitivity, Edna and a team of volunteers have distributed thousands of copies of her works to underprivileged children in India, Africa, and the United States. "Challenging My Ego" has evolved into a curriculum designed for public schools and children's organizations, offering a five-week intensive learning program for the summer or year-round.

Beyond her literary contributions, Edna is a tireless traveler who shares an inspiring message of faith, hope, motivation, and personal growth in every corner of the world. Through her Creative Writing workshops, she fosters a community of writers committed to honoring God with their words. For more information about her work or to invite her to share her message, you can contact her offices or visit her website: www.jdnpublications.com

REFERENCES

Holy Bible, New International Version. (2011). Biblica, Inc. Retrieved from https://www.biblegateway.com

Holy Bible, New King James Version. (1982). Thomas Nelson. Retrieved from https://www.biblegateway.com

Holy Bible, New Living Translation. (2015). Tyndale House Foundation. Retrieved from https://www.biblegateway.com

https://www.google.com/search?q=https://www.cuidatudinero.com/13118952/how-to-extract-separate-and-refine-gold

https://www.google.com/search?q=https://en.oxforddictionaries.com/definition/leaching

Informative Video: Geology of Gold in the World, retrieved December 4, 2018, from www.youtube.com

https://www.google.com/search?q=http://cienciasdelosmaterialesindustrial.blogspot.com/p/copper-red-brown-ductile-metal_2378.html https://www.google.com/search?q=http://outletminero.org/what-is-and-why-is-gold-refining-important/

www.ingramcontent.com/pod-product-compliance
Lightning Source LLC
Chambersburg PA
CBHW061803070526
44586CB00023B/2699